Women in Leadership Rise and Succeed
Essential Leadership Competencies for Women in the Digital Workplace

BY
Blake Jasso

CONTENTS

INTRODUCTION 2

Part 1: 12
Managing Health and Well-being 12

Chapter 01 13
Understanding the Medical Needs of Aging Parents 13
Chapter 02 23
Creating a Safe and Comfortable Living Environment .. 23
Chapter 03 34
Nutrition and Physical Well-being 34
Chapter 04 45
Organizing and Managing Finances 45
Chapter 05 57
Legal Considerations and Important Documents 57

Part 2: 69
Navigating Finances and Legalities 69

Chapter 06 70
Paying for Long-Term Care 70
Chapter 07 80
Coping with the Emotional Challenges of Caregiving ... 80

Part 3: 88
Emotional Support and Caregiver Well-being 88

Chapter 08 89
Maintaining Strong Family Relationships 89
Chapter 09 98
Finding and Utilizing External Support Systems 98

Chapter 10..106
Planning for the Future and End-of-Life Care................106

Conclusion 114

INTRODUCTION

The Rise of Women in Leadership

The path of women in leadership has been long and winding, full of challenges but also marked by remarkable achievements. Women have made significant strides in gaining positions of power, responsibility, and influence, but the road is far from smooth. This introduction explores the shifting landscape of leadership, what inspired this guide, and the challenges and opportunities women face today. If you're a woman aspiring to lead or already in a leadership role, you're about to embark on a journey to strengthen your leadership competencies and thrive in today's digital world.

The Shifting Landscape of Leadership

In recent decades, we've seen a substantial increase in the number of women rising to leadership positions. Women are no longer confined to traditional roles, and the landscape is evolving. In corporate boardrooms, government offices, and startups, women are breaking barriers and redefining what leadership looks like. Today, women are leading multimillion-dollar companies, creating social change, and innovating in industries once considered male-dominated. However, despite this progress, women still face unique challenges that their male counterparts may not experience as often or as acutely.

Glass Ceilings and Gender Pay Gaps

One of the most commonly discussed barriers is the proverbial "glass ceiling." This invisible yet stubborn barrier prevents many women from advancing to the highest levels of leadership, particularly in industries like technology, finance, and politics. Even when women do reach these positions, they often find that they are compensated less than their male peers for the same role and responsibilities. According to numerous studies, gender pay gaps persist, and the representation of women in senior leadership remains far lower than it should be, particularly in top executive roles like CEOs and board chairs.

Social Expectations and Stereotypes

While the glass ceiling may be one of the most prominent barriers, it's far from the only one. Many women also face entrenched social expectations and stereotypes. The perception of women as "nurturers" or "supporters" rather than leaders continues to exist, often making it more challenging for women to be seen as capable and assertive leaders. Women are sometimes expected to balance professional success with family responsibilities in a way that men may not, adding another layer of complexity to their leadership journey.

Progress Amid Challenges

Yet, in the face of these hurdles, progress continues to be made. Women like Mary Barra (CEO of General Motors), Kamala Harris (Vice President of the United States), and other trailblazing leaders have shown what's possible when barriers are overcome. Their success stories serve as inspiration, but they also highlight the fact that achieving such heights often requires overcoming more than just professional challenges—personal, cultural, and systemic hurdles must also be navigated.

This shifting landscape is not only about representation; it's about redefining leadership in ways that are more inclusive, empathetic, and collaborative—qualities that women leaders often exemplify. In fact, research has shown that companies with greater diversity in leadership perform better financially and are more innovative. So, while challenges remain, the opportunity to reshape the future of leadership is real, and women are at the forefront of this transformation.

Why This Book?

"Seeding Faith, Reaping Champions" was born out of a need to provide women with practical, actionable advice on how to rise and succeed in leadership roles, particularly in today's fast-paced, digital workplace. The digital world presents both opportunities and challenges, and women need to be equipped with the right tools to navigate this new environment.

Leadership books often focus on the "what" — what qualities great leaders possess, what skills are essential, and what challenges exist. This book goes further by focusing on the "how" — how you can develop the competencies necessary to thrive, how you can build resilience in the face of adversity, and how you can practically apply leadership principles in your day-to-day life. It's designed to be a resource that you can return to repeatedly, not just for inspiration but for tangible strategies and actions.

Building Leadership Competencies

Competency is at the core of leadership. You may have the ambition to lead, but leadership requires more than ambition — it demands skills, strategies, and the ability to adapt to evolving challenges. This book is a guide to building essential leadership competencies, such as emotional intelligence, communication skills, strategic thinking, and digital literacy, all of which are critical in the modern workplace. It focuses on not just developing these competencies but using them to thrive as a leader, no matter your industry or role.

A Practical, Action-Oriented Approach

One of the key differences with this guide is its focus on action. We're not here to give you a history lesson on women in leadership or to rehash common leadership theories. Instead, we aim to provide actionable steps that you can start applying immediately. Whether it's strategies for building confidence, practical advice on handling difficult conversations, or techniques for balancing work and life, each chapter is designed to equip you with tools you can put into practice right away.

Who This Book Is For

Whether you're a recent college graduate stepping into your first managerial role, a mid-career professional looking to make the jump to senior leadership, or a seasoned executive wanting to sharpen your skills, this book is for you. Women at all stages of their careers can benefit from the competencies outlined here because leadership isn't a static destination—it's a continuous journey.

Aspiring Leaders

If you're just starting out on your leadership journey, you may feel overwhelmed by the expectations and challenges ahead. You may question whether you have what it takes to lead, especially in male-dominated environments. This book will help you build the foundational competencies necessary to not only survive but thrive in leadership roles. From building confidence to developing strong communication skills, we will walk you through the first steps of your leadership journey.

Current Managers and Mid-Level Leaders

For women already in leadership positions, the challenges may be different but no less complex. You may be grappling with how to manage teams, navigate organizational politics, or push for promotions. You may also be struggling with balancing your leadership responsibilities with personal commitments. This book will provide strategies for navigating these complexities while continuing to grow as a leader.

Senior Executives

For experienced leaders, this book serves as a reminder that leadership is an ongoing process of development. No matter how long you've been in a leadership role, there's always room to refine your approach, build new skills, and find innovative ways to inspire your team. In particular, the digital workplace presents unique challenges for senior executives, and this book will offer insights on how to lead effectively in this new landscape.

The Challenges Women Face

While this book is all about empowering women to rise and succeed, it's important to acknowledge the unique challenges that women face on the path to leadership.

These challenges are real, but they are not insurmountable.

Gender Bias

Despite the strides women have made, gender bias continues to exist, often subtly but sometimes overtly. Women are frequently subjected to different standards than their male counterparts, whether in terms of how assertive they're allowed to be, how much emotion they're expected to show, or how competent they're perceived to be. Studies have shown that women's leadership styles are often undervalued, and women are more likely to be interrupted or talked over in meetings. Recognizing and addressing these biases is crucial to overcoming them.

Work-Life Balance

Another major challenge for women leaders is the pressure to balance professional success with personal commitments. Women are often expected to manage both leadership roles and family responsibilities seamlessly, a pressure that men don't face to the same extent. This balancing act can lead to burnout or feelings of inadequacy in one area or the other. However, this book will provide actionable strategies to manage these competing demands, ensuring that you can excel in both your professional and personal lives.

Self-Doubt and Impostor Syndrome

Perhaps one of the most internalized challenges women face is self-doubt. Even highly accomplished women often struggle with what's known as "impostor syndrome" — the belief that they are not as competent or qualified as others perceive them to be, and that they will eventually be "found out" as a fraud. This mindset can be paralyzing, but it doesn't have to define you. Throughout this book, you'll find strategies for overcoming self-doubt and building a strong, resilient sense of self-worth.

What to Expect

Throughout this book, you will find a comprehensive breakdown of core leadership competencies, from emotional intelligence to digital fluency, as well as practical strategies to overcome the challenges women face in leadership. Each chapter is designed to equip you with the tools you need to grow both personally and professionally.

Building Essential Competencies

You'll learn how to cultivate confidence, communicate effectively, build influence, and lead teams with empathy and resilience. These competencies aren't just nice-to-haves; they're essential for any woman looking to rise and succeed in the digital workplace. We'll break down each competency into actionable steps and exercises that you can begin applying immediately.

Overcoming Barriers

Whether it's dealing with gender biases, navigating difficult conversations, or balancing work and life, this book will provide strategies for overcoming the barriers that women commonly face. You'll find advice on how to assert yourself without being labeled as "too aggressive," how to manage the expectations placed on you, and how to cultivate resilience in the face of setbacks.

Tools for Growth and Resilience

Leadership isn't just about achieving success; it's also about growing continuously and remaining resilient in the face of challenges. This book will give you the tools to do both. From developing a growth mindset to building networks of support, you'll find strategies to ensure that your leadership journey is sustainable and fulfilling.

In the pages ahead, we'll dive deep into each of these topics, offering you both insight and action. Leadership isn't just about reaching the top; it's about rising in a way that allows you to succeed, support others, and make a lasting impact. The time is now, and you have the tools to rise and reap the rewards of leadership. Let's begin this journey together.

Part 1:
Building Your Leadership Foundation

Chapter 01

Cultivating Confidence and Building a Leadership Mindset

Confidence is often viewed as the cornerstone of effective leadership. Without it, even the most skilled leaders struggle to gain the trust and respect of their teams. But confidence doesn't just happen overnight—it's built over time, through self-awareness, personal growth, and learning how to bounce back from setbacks. This chapter is designed to help you cultivate the mindset necessary for leadership, tackle impostor syndrome, build resilience, and develop the skills that will set you up for success. Whether you're just beginning your leadership journey or are a seasoned manager looking to sharpen your skills, this chapter will guide you toward a stronger, more confident leadership style.

Developing a Leadership Mindset

Leadership isn't just about being in charge; it's about developing the mindset that allows you to inspire, influence, and guide others toward a common goal. To do this effectively, you must first understand yourself—your strengths, weaknesses, motivations, and how you respond to challenges. Cultivating a leadership mindset involves self-awareness, growth, and a commitment to continuous improvement. Let's break this down into actionable steps.

Self-awareness and Reflection

Self-awareness is the first and most important step in developing a leadership mindset. Before you can lead others, you need to understand who you are as a leader. What are your strengths? What are the areas you need to improve? How do you react under pressure? These are essential questions that will guide your growth.

One effective way to assess your leadership style is through **reflection and journaling**. Set aside time each week to reflect on your leadership experiences. Ask yourself questions like:

- What leadership challenges did I face this week?
- How did I handle them?
- What went well, and what could have been improved?

By regularly reflecting on your actions and reactions, you'll gain deeper insights into your leadership tendencies and identify patterns in your behavior.

Another powerful tool is **360-degree feedback**. This method involves gathering feedback from those around you—your peers, direct reports, and supervisors. It offers a well-rounded view of how others perceive your leadership abilities. Be open to constructive criticism and use it as a foundation for growth. Don't just focus on weaknesses; also celebrate your strengths and think about how you can leverage them to lead more effectively.

Shifting from Impostor Syndrome to Confidence

One of the most pervasive challenges women face in leadership is **impostor syndrome**—the persistent belief that they are not as competent or deserving as others perceive them to be. Even highly accomplished women often struggle with feelings of self-doubt, fearing that they will be "found out" or that their success is due to luck rather than skill.

To combat impostor syndrome, you need to shift your mindset from self-doubt to self-belief. Here are some strategies that can help:

Acknowledge your accomplishments: Start by listing out your achievements, big and small. Keep a journal of successes, milestones, and positive feedback. This practice will help you internalize your accomplishments and build confidence.

Reframe negative thoughts: When self-doubt creeps in, reframe your thinking. Instead of saying, "I'm not qualified for this role," tell yourself, "I have the skills and experience to handle this challenge." Challenge negative thoughts with evidence of your competence.

Affirmations and visualization: Develop positive affirmations to remind yourself of your strengths. Visualize yourself succeeding in leadership scenarios, whether it's giving a presentation, leading a meeting, or negotiating a deal. Visualization primes your brain for success and builds confidence.

Seek out mentors and role models: Surround yourself with people who believe in you. Having a mentor or a supportive peer group can provide a confidence boost, as well as practical advice on how to navigate leadership challenges. They can also offer a reality check when impostor syndrome rears its head.

By practicing these techniques regularly, you'll begin to shift from a mindset of self-doubt to one of confidence. Remember, everyone experiences moments of insecurity—what matters is how you handle them.

Cultivating Resilience and Adaptability

Leadership, particularly in a fast-paced digital world, requires **resilience and adaptability**. Leaders must be able to manage setbacks, bounce back from failures, and adjust to constantly changing environments. Resilience doesn't mean avoiding failure; it means learning from it and continuing to move forward.

Here's how you can cultivate resilience as a leader:

Embrace failure as a learning opportunity: Reframe failures as valuable learning experiences. Instead of seeing them as a reflection of your capabilities, view them as a chance to grow. Ask yourself, "What can I learn from this situation?" and "How can I use this experience to improve?"

Develop emotional regulation skills: In leadership, setbacks and challenges are inevitable. Leaders must be able to manage their emotions in difficult situations. Practice deep breathing, mindfulness, or meditation to stay grounded when faced with stress or pressure. The ability to maintain composure under pressure will earn you the respect of your team and allow you to make more rational decisions.

Adaptability and flexibility: In the digital age, things move fast, and leaders need to be flexible. Be open to change, and don't be afraid to adjust your strategies or pivot when necessary. Adaptability shows strength and foresight, qualities that inspire trust in your team.

Resilience and adaptability are qualities that will serve you well, not only in leadership but in all areas of life. By cultivating these traits, you'll be better equipped to handle the ups and downs that come with leading in today's dynamic workplace.

Growth Mindset for Continuous Learning

The concept of a **growth mindset**, popularized by psychologist Carol Dweck, is essential for leadership development. A growth mindset is the belief that abilities and intelligence can be developed through dedication and hard work. Leaders with a growth mindset see challenges as opportunities to learn and grow, rather than threats to their competence.

In the digital workplace, where change is constant and technology evolves rapidly, a growth mindset is crucial. Here's how to cultivate it:

Embrace challenges: Instead of avoiding difficult tasks or situations, seek them out. Challenges stretch your abilities and push you to grow. The more you expose yourself to new experiences, the more confident you'll become in your capacity to handle them.

Be open to feedback: A key aspect of a growth mindset is being open to constructive criticism. Use feedback as a tool for self-improvement, rather than seeing it as a personal attack. Leaders who actively seek feedback are better positioned to grow and adapt in their roles.

Learn, unlearn, and relearn: The pace of technological change means that some skills you possess today may be obsolete tomorrow. To remain effective, you must be willing to unlearn old habits and relearn new ones. Stay curious, and never stop learning. Take online courses, attend workshops, and stay updated on industry trends.

Celebrate effort, not just results: Shift your focus from solely achieving results to valuing the effort you put into learning and improving. This mindset encourages perseverance and long-term growth.

By adopting a growth mindset, you'll foster a culture of continuous learning within yourself and your team. This mindset not only builds your leadership capacity but also empowers others to strive for growth and innovation.

Confidence Through Preparation

One of the most practical ways to build confidence is through **preparation**. When you're well-prepared, you feel more in control, which directly translates into confidence. Whether it's public speaking, giving presentations, or negotiating, preparation is key to showing up confidently in leadership situations.

Here are some tips for building confidence through preparation:

Public speaking and presentations: If public speaking makes you nervous, practice is your best friend. Rehearse your speeches or presentations multiple times, and if possible, in front of a friend or mentor who can give feedback. The more familiar you are with your material, the more natural and confident you'll feel when delivering it.

Negotiation skills: Confidence in negotiation comes from knowing your worth and being well-prepared. Before entering a negotiation, research your position thoroughly. Know the market rates, understand the interests of the other party, and anticipate potential objections. When you're armed with knowledge, you'll be able to assert yourself confidently and secure better outcomes.

Active listening: Preparation isn't just about what you say; it's also about how you listen. Good leaders are confident because they understand the needs and concerns of their team. Practice active listening by being fully present in conversations and asking clarifying questions. This will not only improve your understanding but also build trust and confidence within your team.

Confidence doesn't come from wishing for it—it comes from being prepared, informed, and ready for the challenges you'll face.

Own Your Leadership Narrative

One of the most empowering things you can do as a leader is to **own your leadership narrative**. Your journey, experiences, and values are what make you unique as a leader. By crafting and communicating your personal leadership story, you can inspire and influence others.

Here's how to develop and share your leadership narrative:

Reflect on your journey: Think about the experiences that have shaped you as a leader. What challenges have you overcome? What values guide your decisions? How have your personal experiences influenced your leadership style? These reflections will form the foundation of your leadership story.

Be authentic: Authenticity is key when sharing your leadership narrative. People are drawn to leaders who are genuine and transparent. Don't be afraid to share your struggles and failures alongside your successes—this vulnerability will make you more relatable and trustworthy.

Use your story to inspire: Your leadership narrative isn't just for you—it's a tool to inspire and motivate others. Whether you're speaking to your team, presenting at a conference, or mentoring a colleague, your story can serve as a powerful example of resilience, growth, and leadership.

Stay consistent: Your leadership narrative should evolve over time, but the core values and principles that define your leadership should remain consistent. By staying true to your story, you'll build a strong, authentic leadership presence.

Owning your leadership narrative allows you to shape how others perceive you and gives you the confidence to lead with purpose and clarity.

In this chapter, we've explored the foundations of cultivating confidence and developing a leadership mindset. From building self-awareness to overcoming impostor syndrome, from cultivating resilience to owning your leadership narrative, these strategies will help you grow as a leader and prepare you for the challenges ahead. Leadership begins in the mind—when you cultivate the right mindset, confidence and success will follow.

Chapter 02

Building Influence and Driving Impact

Leadership is not just about holding a title or being in charge; it's about influence. The ability to influence others is one of the most powerful tools a leader can possess. It's what enables you to drive change, inspire your team, and make a lasting impact within your organization. But influence doesn't happen by accident—it's built through trust, credibility, and effective communication. In this chapter, we will explore the core competencies necessary for building influence and driving impact as a leader, focusing on actionable strategies that will help you establish credibility, cultivate meaningful relationships, and communicate effectively in order to lead with authority and purpose.

Establishing Credibility and Trust

As a leader, **credibility and trust** are the foundation of your influence. Without trust, it's impossible to lead effectively because people won't follow or buy into your vision. Trust is earned over time through consistent actions, integrity, and transparency. Building credibility is equally important—it gives you the authority to make decisions, advocate for change, and lead with confidence.

The Importance of Trust in Leadership

Trust is the currency of leadership. When people trust you, they are more likely to support your decisions, follow your lead, and contribute their best efforts. So how do you build and maintain trust in your leadership?

Be transparent and authentic: People trust leaders who are open and honest. Don't be afraid to be transparent about challenges, changes, or mistakes.

When you're upfront with your team, they'll feel more secure knowing they're getting the full picture. Authenticity—being true to yourself and your values—is equally important. Don't try to be someone you're not just to fit a mold of leadership. When people see that you're genuine, they'll respect you more.

Follow through on commitments: Trust is built through consistent actions. If you promise to do something, make sure you follow through. Whether it's meeting deadlines, addressing team concerns, or delivering on promises to clients, reliability is key to maintaining trust. In cases where you can't meet a commitment, communicate early and often to manage expectations.

Admit mistakes and take accountability: No leader is perfect, and mistakes are inevitable. When you make a mistake, own up to it rather than deflecting blame. Taking responsibility shows humility and integrity, and it builds trust with your team. It also sets an example that it's okay to admit errors and learn from them—an important culture to foster in any team.

Show empathy and listen actively: To build trust, you need to show your team that you genuinely care about them. Practice active listening—when someone speaks to you, give them your full attention. Acknowledge their concerns and feelings, and provide support where possible. Empathy helps create strong connections, and when people feel heard and understood, they are more likely to trust and respect your leadership.

Developing Your Personal Brand

In today's digital workplace, **your personal brand** is a reflection of who you are as a leader. It's how you present yourself to the world—your values, strengths, and leadership vision. A strong personal brand not only builds credibility but also helps you stand out and influence others. Whether you're building a team, seeking a promotion, or networking with industry peers, your personal brand is a key factor in how others perceive you.

Here's how to develop and project a personal brand that reflects your leadership style:

Identify your core values: What do you stand for as a leader? Integrity, innovation, empathy, resilience—your values should guide your actions and decisions. Take time to reflect on what matters most to you and how those values influence your leadership style. Your personal brand should be an authentic reflection of these principles.

Highlight your strengths: Think about what sets you apart from other leaders. What are your unique skills, experiences, or perspectives that add value to your team and organization? Whether it's your expertise in a particular area, your ability to lead diverse teams, or your innovative approach to problem-solving, make sure these strengths are part of your personal brand.

Craft your leadership vision: Your vision is your guiding light as a leader—it's the big-picture impact you want to make. Whether your vision is to foster innovation, build a more inclusive workplace, or lead your team to industry leadership, make it a central part of your brand. This vision will inspire others and attract like-minded individuals who share your goals.

Be consistent across platforms: Your personal brand should be consistent in everything you do—whether it's in the workplace, on social media, or at industry events. Make sure your messaging, behavior, and online presence all align with the brand you want to project. Consistency builds trust and reinforces your credibility as a leader.

By intentionally cultivating your personal brand, you can create a strong, authentic presence that positions you as a leader of influence in your field.

Building Relationships and Networks

One of the most valuable tools for building influence is **networking**—not just for career advancement but also for establishing relationships that can drive long-term success. Strong networks provide access to opportunities, support, and resources that are critical for leadership development. In a digital and interconnected world, networking has become more important than ever.

Here's how to approach networking as a strategic tool for leadership success:

Build meaningful connections: Networking isn't just about collecting business cards or LinkedIn connections; it's about building genuine relationships.

Take the time to get to know people on a deeper level. What are their goals, challenges, and values? How can you help them? When you focus on building mutually beneficial relationships, your network becomes a source of support and collaboration rather than just a collection of contacts.

Seek out mentors and sponsors: A mentor is someone who offers guidance, advice, and support as you navigate your career. A sponsor, on the other hand, is someone who actively advocates for you, opening doors and helping you advance within your organization. Both are crucial to your leadership development. Identify people who can provide mentorship and sponsorship, and nurture these relationships. Be open to learning from their experiences and take advantage of the opportunities they provide.

Network within and outside your organization: Don't limit your networking to people within your company. Industry events, conferences, and professional associations offer opportunities to connect with peers, thought leaders, and potential collaborators outside your organization. These connections can provide fresh perspectives, new ideas, and potential partnerships that drive innovation and impact.

Give back to your network: Networking is a two-way street. Be generous with your time, advice, and resources. Offer support to others in your network when they need it. By building a reputation as someone who is helpful and collaborative, you'll strengthen your relationships and enhance your influence within your network.

By cultivating meaningful relationships and leveraging your network strategically, you'll create opportunities for yourself and others while building a foundation of influence that extends beyond your immediate circle.

Inclusive Leadership

Today's workplaces are more diverse than ever, and **inclusive leadership** is essential for driving innovation, engagement, and success. As a leader, you have the power to create environments where every voice is heard, valued, and empowered to contribute. Inclusive leadership isn't just about diversity in numbers; it's about fostering a culture of belonging where everyone feels respected and included.

Here are key strategies for becoming a more inclusive leader:

Embrace diversity: Diversity goes beyond race and gender—it includes differences in background, experience, perspectives, and ideas. Embrace this diversity by actively seeking out and valuing different viewpoints. Encourage diverse thinking within your team and create opportunities for all members to contribute their unique strengths.

Lead with empathy: Empathy is at the heart of inclusive leadership. Take the time to understand the experiences, challenges, and needs of your team members. Listen to their concerns and be proactive in addressing any barriers they may face. Empathetic leaders build trust and create a culture where people feel comfortable sharing their ideas and concerns.

Foster psychological safety: Psychological safety is the belief that you can speak up, share ideas, and make mistakes without fear of retribution. As a leader, it's your job to create a safe space where team members feel comfortable taking risks and being themselves. Encourage open dialogue, support experimentation, and celebrate learning from failure.

Ensure equitable opportunities: Inclusive leaders are mindful of the opportunities they provide for their team members. Make sure that everyone has access to the same opportunities for development, growth, and advancement. Be proactive in addressing any biases—whether conscious or unconscious—that may affect decision-making or hinder the progress of underrepresented groups.

By leading inclusively, you'll not only foster a positive and productive team culture but also enhance your influence by demonstrating a commitment to fairness, equity, and respect.

Effective Communication Strategies

Communication is one of the most critical skills for any leader. It's not just about what you say but how you say it. Effective communication involves understanding your audience, tailoring your message, and mastering both verbal and non-verbal cues. In today's digital workplace, where communication often happens across multiple platforms, mastering these skills is essential for building influence and driving impact.

Here's how to improve your communication skills as a leader:

Tailor your message for different audiences: Different audiences require different communication approaches. When speaking to executives, focus on high-level strategy and outcomes. When addressing your team, be clear about expectations and provide the context they need to do their jobs effectively. When communicating with clients or stakeholders, emphasize how your solutions align with their needs and goals. Adapt your message to meet the expectations and interests of each group.

Master non-verbal communication: Your body language, facial expressions, and tone of voice all convey powerful messages. Make sure your non-verbal cues align with your verbal message. For example, maintaining eye contact shows confidence and engagement, while a strong posture conveys authority. Be mindful of these cues, especially in virtual meetings where body language can sometimes be harder to read.

Listen more than you speak: Effective communication is a two-way street. Listening is just as important as speaking, if not more so. Practice active listening by giving your full attention to the speaker, asking clarifying questions, and acknowledging their points. This shows respect and helps you better understand the needs and concerns of others.

Communicate across digital platforms: In the digital workplace, communication often happens through emails, video calls, and messaging platforms.

Each medium has its own set of best practices. For example, emails should be clear and concise, while video calls require strong presence and engagement. Develop the skills to communicate effectively across different platforms, and always be mindful of tone and clarity, especially in written communication where non-verbal cues are absent.

Provide constructive feedback: Feedback is a critical part of leadership communication. When providing feedback, focus on being specific, constructive, and solution-oriented. Avoid criticism that is vague or overly negative. Instead, highlight areas for improvement while offering actionable suggestions for growth. This type of feedback helps individuals improve while maintaining motivation and morale.

In this chapter, we've covered essential strategies for building influence and driving impact as a leader. From establishing credibility and developing a strong personal brand to building relationships, practicing inclusive leadership, and mastering communication, these competencies will help you lead with authority and purpose. Influence is not about power or control—it's about building trust, creating meaningful connections, and inspiring others to work toward a shared vision.

Chapter 03

Building a Personal Brand as a Female Leader

In today's professional world, building a personal brand is essential for leadership success, especially for women who are looking to stand out in the workplace. Your personal brand is a reflection of who you are, what you stand for, and how others perceive you. As a female leader, cultivating a strong personal brand can help you gain visibility, earn respect, and open doors to new opportunities. This chapter will guide you through the process of building and refining your personal brand, aligning it with your values, leveraging social media, and ensuring visibility in your organization and industry.

What is a Personal Brand, and Why Does It Matter?

A personal brand is the unique combination of skills, experiences, values, and personality that you bring to the table as a leader. It's how others see you and what they think of when your name comes up. Personal branding isn't just for entrepreneurs or influencers; it's crucial for anyone looking to rise in their career, especially in leadership roles. For women, building a strong personal brand is particularly important because it can help overcome gender bias and stereotypes, allowing you to stand out for your skills and accomplishments rather than just fitting into preconceived notions of leadership.

Why Personal Branding Matters for Female Leaders:

- **Establishes Authority**: A strong personal brand helps establish you as a thought leader and expert in your field. This authority boosts your credibility and

influence, both inside your organization and in the broader industry.
- **Increases Visibility**: In competitive workplaces, visibility is key to advancing your career. A well-defined personal brand ensures that your contributions are noticed and recognized.
- **Shapes Perception**: Whether you actively manage your personal brand or not, others are forming opinions about you. By proactively shaping your brand, you control how people perceive you and ensure that your image aligns with your goals and values.
- **Attracts Opportunities**: A clear, compelling personal brand can attract new opportunities for growth, including promotions, partnerships, speaking engagements, and leadership roles.
- **Differentiates You**: In a crowded field, your personal brand sets you apart from others. It highlights what makes you unique and helps others understand why they should choose you for a leadership role or collaboration.

By defining and promoting your personal brand, you create a strong foundation for long-term leadership success.

Aligning Your Values and Strengths with Your Brand

Before you can effectively build a personal brand, you need to understand your core values and strengths. Your personal brand should be an authentic reflection of who you are as a leader, so aligning your brand with your values is critical. This alignment not only makes your brand more genuine but also makes it easier to consistently live up to the image you project.

Steps to Align Your Values and Strengths with Your Brand:

Identify Your Core Values: What are the guiding principles that influence your decisions and actions? Whether it's integrity, innovation, empathy, or collaboration, your values should form the foundation of your brand. Start by listing out the values that matter most to you in both your professional and personal life.

Assess Your Strengths: Take time to reflect on your key strengths and skills. What do you excel at? What do others frequently compliment you on? These strengths are integral to your brand. Consider how these skills differentiate you as a leader and make you valuable to your organization and industry.

Determine Your Leadership Style: Think about how you lead and manage teams. Are you collaborative, strategic, or inspirational? Your leadership style is a key component of your personal brand, and it should align with the image you want to project.

Define Your Unique Selling Proposition (USP): Your USP is what sets you apart from others in your field. It's the combination of your strengths, skills, and values that makes you a unique and valuable leader. Ask yourself: "What do I offer that others don't?" Your USP should be at the heart of your personal brand.

Ensure Consistency: Consistency is key to building a strong personal brand. Your actions, communication, and decisions should consistently reflect your values and strengths. When your brand is aligned with who you truly are, it becomes easier to maintain and grow over time.

By aligning your values, strengths, and leadership style with your personal brand, you create a powerful, authentic presence that resonates with others and strengthens your leadership position.

How to Leverage Social Media and Networking for Personal Brand Growth

In today's digital age, social media and networking are powerful tools for building and promoting your personal brand. As a female leader, leveraging these platforms effectively can help you gain visibility, expand your network, and establish yourself as an authority in your field. However, using social media and networking strategically is key to ensuring that your online presence supports your leadership goals.

Leveraging Social Media for Personal Branding:

Choose the Right Platforms: Not all social media platforms are created equal, and you don't need to be on every single one. Focus on platforms that align with your professional goals and audience. LinkedIn is essential for professional branding, while Twitter and Instagram can be valuable for thought leadership and connecting with industry peers.

Create a Professional and Engaging Profile: Your social media profiles are often the first impression others will have of your personal brand. Ensure that your profiles are professional, up-to-date, and consistent across platforms. Use a high-quality photo, write a compelling bio, and highlight your accomplishments and leadership experience.

Share Thought Leadership Content: One of the best ways to establish yourself as an authority in your field is by sharing content that demonstrates your expertise. This could include writing articles or blog posts, sharing industry news, commenting on trends, or even posting videos or webinars. Focus on providing value to your audience and positioning yourself as a knowledgeable leader.

Engage with Your Audience: Social media isn't just about broadcasting your message—it's about engaging in meaningful conversations. Take the time to comment on others' posts, respond to messages, and participate in discussions within your industry. Building relationships online can lead to valuable connections and opportunities.

Stay Authentic: While it's important to maintain professionalism, don't be afraid to show your personality and share your authentic self. People are drawn to leaders who are relatable and genuine, so find a balance between showcasing your expertise and being approachable.

Networking for Personal Brand Growth:

Expand Your Professional Network: Networking is crucial for leadership success. Attend industry events, join professional organizations, and participate in conferences or workshops to expand your network. The more people you connect with, the more opportunities you have to build your personal brand.

Build Meaningful Relationships: Networking isn't just about collecting business cards; it's about building meaningful relationships. Take the time to get to know the people you meet, offer support, and stay in touch regularly. These relationships can become valuable advocates for your personal brand.

Leverage Online Networking: In addition to in-person events, online networking can be a powerful tool for growing your brand. Platforms like LinkedIn allow you to connect with industry leaders, potential mentors, and peers from around the world. Don't hesitate to reach out to others, join relevant groups, and participate in online discussions.

Seek Mentorship and Sponsorship: Mentors and sponsors can play a significant role in helping you build your personal brand. Mentors provide guidance and advice, while sponsors actively advocate for your advancement. Building strong relationships with both can help you navigate your leadership journey and enhance your visibility.

Crafting Your Leadership Story: Communicating What Sets You Apart

Every leader has a unique story, and crafting your leadership story is a key part of building your personal brand. Your story is a powerful tool that communicates who you are, what you stand for, and how you've arrived at your current leadership position. It allows you to connect with others on a personal level and differentiate yourself from other leaders.

Steps to Craft Your Leadership Story:

Reflect on Your Journey: Start by reflecting on your career journey. What experiences have shaped you as a leader? What challenges have you overcome? What successes have you achieved? Your story should include the key moments that have defined your leadership path.

Highlight Your Values and Strengths: Your leadership story should align with the values and strengths you've identified as part of your personal brand. Make sure these elements are woven throughout your story to create a consistent and authentic narrative.

Show Vulnerability and Growth: Don't be afraid to share the challenges and failures you've faced along the way. Showing vulnerability and how you've grown from setbacks can make your story more relatable and inspiring to others.

Focus on Impact: Your leadership story isn't just about your experiences—it's about the impact you've made on others. Highlight the positive changes you've brought to your organization, team, or industry, and emphasize how your leadership has contributed to meaningful outcomes.

Practice Telling Your Story: Once you've crafted your leadership story, practice telling it. Whether it's during networking events, interviews, or speaking engagements, being able to articulate your story clearly and confidently is essential for building your brand.

Building Visibility in Your Organization and Industry

As a female leader, visibility is key to advancing your career and strengthening your personal brand. It's not enough to be competent at your job—you need to make sure that others recognize your contributions and see you as a leader. By building visibility in both your organization and your industry, you increase your influence, expand your opportunities, and position yourself for future leadership roles.

Strategies for Building Visibility in Your Organization:

Take on High-Profile Projects: One of the best ways to gain visibility in your organization is by taking on high-profile projects that align with your strengths and leadership goals. Seek out opportunities where you can showcase your skills, make a significant impact, and demonstrate your leadership capabilities.

Speak Up in Meetings: Don't hesitate to share your ideas and opinions in meetings, especially when it comes to topics where you have expertise. Speaking up confidently not only builds your visibility but also positions you as a thought leader within your organization.

Volunteer for Leadership Roles: Whether it's leading a team, heading up a task force, or organizing an internal event, volunteer for leadership roles that allow you to demonstrate your capabilities and build relationships with key decision-makers.

Build Relationships with Senior Leaders: Building relationships with senior leaders in your organization is essential for gaining visibility. Look for opportunities to connect with executives, whether it's through mentorship, networking, or collaborative projects.

Managing Your Brand During Times of Change or Transition

Leadership often comes with times of change or transition, whether it's a new job, a promotion, or a shift in your industry. During these times, managing your personal brand becomes even more important to ensure that you maintain your reputation and continue to grow as a leader.

Strategies for Managing Your Brand in Times of Change:

Stay True to Your Core Values: During times of change, it can be tempting to adapt your personal brand to fit new circumstances. However, staying true to your core values is essential for maintaining authenticity and ensuring that your brand remains consistent.

Communicate Clearly and Proactively: When going through a transition, clear and proactive communication is key. Make sure to communicate your goals, intentions, and progress to key stakeholders to avoid misunderstandings and ensure that your brand remains strong.

Adapt Your Brand to New Opportunities: While it's important to stay true to your core values, it's also essential to adapt your brand to new opportunities. Consider how you can leverage your existing strengths to succeed in new roles or industries, and be open to evolving your brand as your leadership journey progresses.

Seek Feedback: During times of change, seek feedback from trusted mentors or colleagues to ensure that your personal brand is being perceived positively. This feedback can help you make necessary adjustments and ensure that you continue to grow as a leader.

In this chapter, we've explored how to build a personal brand as a female leader, aligning it with your values, leveraging social media and networking, and managing your brand during times of change. Your personal brand is a powerful tool for establishing yourself as a leader, gaining visibility, and attracting new opportunities. By actively managing and growing your brand, you can rise and thrive as a leader in the modern workplace.

Chapter 04
Leading with Integrity and Purpose

Leadership is not just about achieving results; it's about how you achieve those results. Leading with integrity and purpose means aligning your actions with your values, fostering trust within your team, and making ethical decisions that reflect a strong moral compass. This chapter explores the significance of values-driven leadership, how to establish a personal leadership philosophy, and practical steps for leading authentically.

Understanding the Importance of Values-Driven Leadership

Values-driven leadership is essential in creating a positive and productive organizational culture. When leaders prioritize their values, they set a standard for their teams, influencing behaviors and decisions that promote a sense of purpose and direction.

Key Aspects of Values-Driven Leadership:

- **Sets a Clear Vision**: Values-driven leaders create a vision that resonates with their team and aligns with organizational goals. This vision helps guide decision-making and encourages team members to work toward common objectives.
- **Builds Trust and Loyalty**: When leaders act in accordance with their values, they foster trust within their teams. Trust enhances collaboration, encourages open communication, and increases employee engagement.
- **Attracts Like-Minded Individuals**: A strong values-driven culture attracts employees who share similar principles. This alignment enhances team

cohesion and strengthens the overall organizational culture.
- **Facilitates Ethical Decision-Making**: Leaders who prioritize their values are more likely to make ethical decisions, even in challenging situations. This commitment to integrity strengthens the organization's reputation and fosters a positive work environment.

By leading with integrity and purpose, you not only contribute to a healthy organizational culture but also set an example for others to follow.

Establishing a Personal Leadership Philosophy

A personal leadership philosophy serves as your guiding framework for decision-making and interactions with your team. It defines your values, beliefs, and principles, helping you lead with consistency and authenticity.

Steps to Establish Your Personal Leadership Philosophy:

Reflect on Your Values: Begin by identifying your core values. What principles guide your actions and decisions? Take time to reflect on moments in your life that have shaped your values, both personally and professionally.

Define Your Leadership Beliefs: Consider what you believe about leadership. Do you prioritize collaboration, innovation, or accountability? Write down your beliefs about what makes an effective leader.

Articulate Your Vision: Your leadership philosophy should include a clear vision of what you hope to achieve as a leader. What impact do you want to have on your team and organization? This vision will serve as a roadmap for your leadership journey.

Create a Written Statement: Once you've reflected on your values, beliefs, and vision, craft a concise written statement that encapsulates your personal leadership philosophy. This statement will serve as a constant reminder of your commitment to leading with integrity and purpose.

Regularly Revisit and Revise: Your leadership philosophy is not static; it should evolve as you grow and gain new experiences. Regularly revisit your philosophy to ensure it remains relevant and reflective of your current values and beliefs.

How to Lead Authentically and Foster Trust Within Your Team

Authenticity in leadership is about being true to yourself and leading from a place of genuine belief and conviction. When you lead authentically, you create an environment where team members feel safe to express themselves, share ideas, and take risks.

Strategies for Leading Authentically:

Be Open and Honest: Transparency is key to authentic leadership. Share your thoughts, ideas, and even your uncertainties with your team. This openness fosters trust and encourages team members to do the same.

Encourage Vulnerability: As a leader, it's important to show vulnerability. Share your challenges and experiences, demonstrating that everyone faces obstacles. This approach not only humanizes you but also fosters a culture of openness.

Listen Actively: Active listening is a critical component of authentic leadership. Make an effort to listen to your team members' ideas and concerns without interrupting or dismissing their input. Show that you value their perspectives.

Recognize Contributions: Acknowledge the contributions of your team members regularly. Celebrating their successes fosters a sense of belonging and encourages continued engagement.

Lead by Example: Model the behavior you expect from your team. By demonstrating integrity, accountability, and commitment to your values, you set the standard for your team members to follow.

By leading authentically, you create a culture of trust, collaboration, and engagement, which ultimately enhances team performance and morale.

Balancing Transparency with Professional Boundaries

While transparency is important, maintaining professional boundaries is equally crucial. Striking the right balance ensures that you create a culture of openness while protecting both yourself and your team from potential pitfalls.

Tips for Balancing Transparency and Professional Boundaries:

Share Relevant Information: Be transparent about decisions and changes that affect your team, but avoid oversharing personal details or confidential information. Keep the focus on what is relevant to their work and the organization.

Set Clear Expectations: Communicate your expectations regarding professional conduct and boundaries within the team. Make it clear what information should be shared and what should remain confidential.

Respect Privacy: While it's important to foster openness, be mindful of your team members' privacy. Avoid prying into personal matters unless they choose to share.

Model Appropriate Boundaries: As a leader, you set the tone for professional boundaries. Ensure you maintain a level of professionalism in your interactions and encourage your team to do the same.

Encourage Open Dialogue: Create opportunities for team members to express their concerns or ask questions. Foster an environment where they feel comfortable discussing boundaries and transparency.

By balancing transparency with professional boundaries, you create a culture that encourages open communication while maintaining a respectful and professional atmosphere.

The Role of Ethics in Decision-Making and Leadership Actions

Ethics play a crucial role in leadership, shaping the decisions you make and the actions you take. As a leader, you have the responsibility to model ethical behavior and ensure that your decisions align with your values and the greater good of your organization.

Key Considerations for Ethical Leadership:

Define Ethical Standards: Establish clear ethical standards that guide your decision-making processes. Consider the impact of your decisions on your team, organization, and stakeholders.

Involve Your Team in Ethical Discussions: Encourage open discussions about ethics and integrity within your team. Create a safe space for team members to voice their concerns or dilemmas they may encounter.

Evaluate Decisions Through an Ethical Lens: When faced with difficult decisions, evaluate the potential consequences through an ethical lens. Ask yourself: "Does this align with my values? How will it impact my team and organization?"

Lead by Example: Demonstrate ethical behavior in all aspects of your leadership. By modeling integrity and accountability, you set the standard for your team and encourage them to act ethically.

Recognize Ethical Dilemmas: Be aware of potential ethical dilemmas and navigate them thoughtfully. Ensure that your team understands the importance of making ethical choices, even when faced with challenges.

By prioritizing ethics in your decision-making and leadership actions, you build a foundation of trust and respect within your team, creating a positive organizational culture.

Cultivating Accountability Within Yourself and Your Team

Accountability is a cornerstone of effective leadership. As a leader, you must hold yourself accountable for your actions and decisions while fostering a culture of accountability within your team.

Strategies for Cultivating Accountability:

Set Clear Goals and Expectations: Clearly define goals and expectations for yourself and your team. Ensure that everyone understands their roles and responsibilities, creating a shared sense of ownership.

Encourage Self-Reflection: Promote self-reflection within your team by encouraging members to assess their performance regularly. This practice helps individuals take ownership of their contributions and learn from their experiences.

Provide Constructive Feedback: Offer regular feedback to your team members, both positive and constructive. Ensure that feedback is specific, actionable, and focused on improvement.

Acknowledge Mistakes: As a leader, be willing to acknowledge your own mistakes and take responsibility for them. Encourage your team to do the same, creating a safe environment for learning and growth.

Celebrate Accountability: Recognize and celebrate instances of accountability within your team. Highlight individuals who take ownership of their work and make ethical decisions, reinforcing the importance of accountability.

By cultivating accountability within yourself and your team, you foster a culture of trust, collaboration, and continuous improvement, ultimately enhancing team performance and achieving organizational goals.

In this chapter, we've explored the importance of leading with integrity and purpose, establishing a personal leadership philosophy, and fostering trust within your team. By prioritizing values-driven leadership, ethical decision-making, and accountability, you can create a positive organizational culture that empowers your team to thrive. In the next chapter, we will delve into effective strategies for leading diverse teams and harnessing the power of inclusion.

Chapter 05

Navigating Gender Bias and Workplace Politics

In today's professional landscape, women often face unique challenges, including gender bias and workplace politics. Understanding these dynamics and developing effective strategies to navigate them is essential for female leaders aiming to thrive in their careers. This chapter explores common forms of gender bias, provides actionable strategies for overcoming obstacles, and emphasizes the importance of building support networks and advocating for oneself and others.

Recognizing Common Forms of Gender Bias in the Workplace

Gender bias can manifest in various forms, often subtly and insidiously. Recognizing these biases is the first step toward addressing them effectively.

Common Forms of Gender Bias:

- **Stereotyping**: Women are often stereotyped as less competent or less committed to their careers compared to their male counterparts. These stereotypes can influence hiring, promotions, and team dynamics.
- **Performance Evaluation Bias**: Research shows that women's contributions are often undervalued during performance reviews. They may receive less credit for their achievements or be judged more harshly for mistakes.
- **Microaggressions**: These are subtle, often unintentional comments or actions that convey bias or prejudice. For example, asking a woman if she is

"the assistant" rather than acknowledging her leadership role.
- **Tokenism**: Women may be placed in leadership roles as a token gesture, leading to the perception that they are not genuinely qualified for their positions.
- **Exclusion from Networks**: Women may find themselves excluded from informal networks or decision-making processes, limiting their access to opportunities and resources.

By understanding these common forms of gender bias, female leaders can better recognize when they encounter bias and develop strategies to address it.

How to Deal with Microaggressions and Subtle Discrimination

Microaggressions and subtle discrimination can be challenging to address because they are often unrecognized by those who perpetuate them. However, there are effective strategies for dealing with these situations.

Strategies for Addressing Microaggressions:

Stay Calm and Composed: When confronted with a microaggression, take a moment to collect your thoughts. Responding calmly and composedly can help defuse the situation and allow for constructive dialogue.

Address It Directly: If you feel comfortable, address the comment or behavior directly with the individual.

Use "I" statements to express how their words made you feel, such as "I felt dismissed when you said…". This approach fosters a more open conversation.

Seek Clarification: Sometimes, it's beneficial to ask for clarification. Questions like, "What did you mean by that?" can prompt the person to reflect on their words and consider the implications.

Document the Incident: Keep a record of any microaggressions or discriminatory comments you encounter. Documentation can be useful if you decide to escalate the situation or seek support from HR or leadership.

Find Allies: Share your experiences with trusted colleagues or friends who can offer support. They may have faced similar situations and can provide valuable perspective and advice.

Report When Necessary: If microaggressions become a pattern or escalate to more severe forms of discrimination, consider reporting the behavior to HR or a trusted supervisor. It's essential to address systemic issues to create a healthier work environment.

By using these strategies, you can effectively navigate microaggressions and subtle discrimination while fostering a culture of respect and inclusion in the workplace.

Strategies for Breaking Through the Glass Ceiling

The "glass ceiling" refers to the invisible barriers that prevent women from advancing to senior leadership positions. While breaking through these barriers can be challenging, there are actionable strategies to help women achieve their career goals.

Tips for Breaking Through the Glass Ceiling:

Set Clear Career Goals: Define your career aspirations and create a roadmap for achieving them. Set specific, measurable, achievable, relevant, and time-bound (SMART) goals that will guide your journey.

Seek Leadership Opportunities: Actively seek out leadership roles and projects that align with your career goals. Volunteer for high-visibility assignments that showcase your skills and contributions.

Develop Key Skills: Invest in your professional development by acquiring skills that are essential for leadership roles. This may include improving your public speaking, negotiation, or strategic planning abilities.

Find a Mentor or Sponsor: Building relationships with mentors and sponsors can provide valuable guidance and advocacy. A mentor can offer advice and support, while a sponsor can actively promote your achievements and help you navigate organizational politics.

Network Strategically: Build a strong professional network by attending industry events, joining professional organizations, and connecting with other leaders. Networking can open doors to new opportunities and collaborations.

Advocate for Yourself: Don't shy away from promoting your accomplishments and seeking recognition for your contributions. Practice self-advocacy by confidently sharing your successes and aspirations with your peers and leadership.

Stay Resilient: Breaking through the glass ceiling may take time and persistence. Embrace setbacks as learning opportunities and remain focused on your goals, even in the face of challenges.

By employing these strategies, you can effectively navigate the barriers to advancement and work toward achieving your leadership aspirations.

Navigating Workplace Politics with Integrity and Purpose

Workplace politics often involves navigating complex relationships and power dynamics. As a female leader, it's crucial to approach these challenges with integrity and purpose.

Tips for Navigating Workplace Politics:

Build Genuine Relationships: Focus on building authentic relationships with colleagues, superiors, and stakeholders. Take the time to understand their perspectives and motivations, which can enhance collaboration and trust.

Stay Informed: Keep yourself informed about organizational dynamics, changes, and key decision-makers. Understanding the landscape will help you navigate workplace politics more effectively.

Maintain Professionalism: Approach workplace politics with professionalism and integrity. Avoid gossip or negative behavior, and instead focus on constructive conversations and solutions.

Align with Organizational Goals: Ensure that your actions and decisions align with the overall goals of the organization. Demonstrating your commitment to the organization's success can enhance your credibility and influence.

Be Transparent: Foster open communication with your team and colleagues. Being transparent about your intentions and decisions builds trust and reduces misunderstandings.

Lead by Example: Model the behavior you want to see in your workplace. By demonstrating integrity and purpose, you inspire others to act similarly, creating a positive culture.

Navigating workplace politics with integrity and purpose allows you to build trust and credibility, ultimately enhancing your influence as a leader.

Building Alliances and Support Networks to Overcome Obstacles

Building alliances and support networks is vital for overcoming the challenges women face in leadership. These connections can provide encouragement, resources, and opportunities for collaboration.

Strategies for Building Alliances:

Identify Key Allies: Identify individuals within your organization or industry who share similar values and goals. Look for mentors, sponsors, and colleagues who can offer support and guidance.

Join Professional Organizations: Participate in professional associations and networks that focus on women in leadership. These organizations provide valuable resources, networking opportunities, and platforms for advocacy.

Attend Networking Events: Actively participate in networking events, conferences, and workshops to connect with other leaders. Building relationships with peers can lead to new opportunities and collaborations.

Collaborate on Projects: Seek opportunities to collaborate with colleagues on projects or initiatives. Working together fosters relationships and allows you to share knowledge and resources.

Leverage Social Media: Utilize social media platforms, such as LinkedIn, to connect with other professionals and build your network. Share your insights, participate in discussions, and engage with industry leaders to expand your reach.

Offer Support to Others: Building alliances is a two-way street. Offer your support and expertise to others in your network, fostering reciprocal relationships that benefit all parties.

By cultivating strong alliances and support networks, you can navigate obstacles more effectively and create a collaborative environment that empowers women leaders.

Advocating for Yourself and Others in Leadership Discussions

Advocating for yourself and others is essential for driving change and promoting diversity in leadership discussions. As a female leader, it's important to confidently voice your ideas and ensure that women's contributions are recognized and valued.

Tips for Effective Advocacy:

Prepare Thoroughly: Before entering leadership discussions, prepare by gathering data, insights, and examples that support your viewpoints. Being well-informed boosts your confidence and credibility.

Use Clear and Assertive Communication: Communicate your ideas clearly and assertively. Use confident body language, maintain eye contact, and articulate your points effectively to convey your message.

Highlight Contributions of Others: In discussions, ensure that you acknowledge and advocate for the contributions of other women and underrepresented groups. This fosters an inclusive environment and demonstrates your commitment to diversity.

Seek Diverse Perspectives: Encourage diverse viewpoints during discussions. Invite input from team members and colleagues to create a collaborative atmosphere where everyone feels valued.

Follow Up: After discussions, follow up with key stakeholders to reinforce your points and keep the conversation going. This persistence can lead to tangible changes and advancements.

Be a Role Model: By advocating for yourself and others, you set a positive example for your team and colleagues. Encourage them to speak up and share their ideas, creating a culture of advocacy within your organization.

By effectively advocating for yourself and others, you contribute to a more equitable and inclusive workplace where diverse voices are heard and valued.

In this chapter, we've examined the challenges of navigating gender bias and workplace politics, along with practical strategies for overcoming these obstacles. By recognizing bias, addressing microaggressions, building alliances, and advocating for yourself and others, you empower yourself and your team to thrive in the modern workplace. In the next chapter, we will explore effective strategies for leading diverse teams and fostering an inclusive environment.

Part 2:
Leading Teams and Organizations

Chapter 06

Building High-Performing Teams

Creating a high-performing team is essential for achieving organizational goals and fostering a positive workplace culture. High-performing teams are characterized by collaboration, trust, and a shared commitment to excellence. This chapter explores strategies for fostering a culture of collaboration and inclusion, effective delegation, meaningful feedback, motivation, conflict resolution, and creating psychological safety.

How to Foster a Culture of Collaboration and Inclusion

A collaborative and inclusive culture enhances creativity, productivity, and job satisfaction. When team members feel valued and included, they are more likely to contribute their best work.

Strategies for Fostering Collaboration and Inclusion:

Encourage Open Communication: Promote a culture where team members feel comfortable sharing their ideas and opinions. Create regular forums for discussion, such as team meetings or brainstorming sessions, where everyone's input is valued.

Set Clear Goals: Establish shared team goals that align with organizational objectives. When team members understand how their contributions fit into the larger picture, they are more likely to work collaboratively toward achieving those goals.

Celebrate Diversity: Recognize and celebrate the diverse backgrounds and perspectives of your team members. Encourage them to share their unique experiences and insights, fostering a culture of appreciation and inclusion.

Promote Team-Building Activities: Organize team-building exercises that encourage collaboration and relationship-building. Activities can range from professional development workshops to informal social gatherings.

Provide Resources for Collaboration: Equip your team with the tools and resources they need to collaborate effectively. This may include project management software, communication platforms, and collaborative workspaces.

Model Inclusive Behavior: As a leader, demonstrate inclusive behavior by actively engaging with all team members. Acknowledge their contributions and encourage them to participate in discussions and decision-making.

By fostering a culture of collaboration and inclusion, you empower your team to leverage their diverse strengths and work together effectively.

The Keys to Effective Delegation and Trust-Building

Effective delegation is crucial for maximizing team productivity and fostering a sense of ownership among team members. Building trust through delegation not only empowers individuals but also strengthens the overall team dynamic.

Tips for Effective Delegation:

Know Your Team's Strengths: Understand the unique skills and strengths of each team member. Delegating tasks based on individual strengths enhances performance and encourages professional growth.

Set Clear Expectations: Clearly communicate the objectives, deadlines, and expectations associated with the delegated tasks. Ensure that team members understand the desired outcomes and the importance of their contributions.

Provide Autonomy: Give team members the freedom to approach tasks in their own way. Allowing autonomy fosters creativity and demonstrates trust in their abilities.

Check-In Without Micromanaging: Schedule regular check-ins to assess progress and provide support without micromanaging. This approach allows team members to feel supported while maintaining their independence.

Acknowledge Efforts and Outcomes: Recognize and celebrate the efforts and achievements of team members following delegation. This acknowledgment reinforces trust and encourages future collaboration.

Encourage Feedback: Create an environment where team members feel comfortable providing feedback on the delegation process. This two-way communication strengthens relationships and improves future delegations.

Effective delegation fosters trust within the team, leading to enhanced performance and a greater sense of ownership.

Providing Meaningful Feedback That Drives Performance

Feedback is a powerful tool for driving performance and professional development. Providing meaningful feedback encourages growth, enhances skills, and fosters a culture of continuous improvement.

Best Practices for Providing Meaningful Feedback:

Be Specific and Actionable: When giving feedback, be specific about what was done well and what could be improved. Use concrete examples to illustrate your points and provide actionable suggestions for improvement.

Use the "Sandwich" Method: Frame feedback using the "sandwich" approach: start with positive feedback, follow with constructive criticism, and conclude with another positive comment. This method helps soften the impact of criticism and maintains motivation.

Make Feedback Timely: Provide feedback as close to the event as possible. Timely feedback is more relevant and allows team members to make immediate adjustments.

Encourage Self-Reflection: Invite team members to reflect on their own performance. Asking open-ended questions, such as "What do you think went well?" or "What could you have done differently?" encourages self-assessment and accountability.

Focus on Development: Frame feedback as an opportunity for growth. Emphasize how constructive criticism can lead to skill enhancement and increased effectiveness.

Create a Feedback Culture: Encourage a culture of open feedback where team members feel comfortable giving and receiving feedback. Regularly solicit feedback from your team to foster continuous improvement.

By providing meaningful feedback, you help team members develop their skills and enhance overall team performance.

The Art of Motivating and Inspiring Diverse Teams

Motivating and inspiring a diverse team requires an understanding of individual and collective needs. Tailoring your approach to motivation can lead to higher engagement and productivity.

Strategies for Motivating Diverse Teams:

Understand Individual Motivations: Take the time to learn what motivates each team member. Individual motivations may vary based on career goals, personal values, and work styles.

Align Tasks with Passions: Whenever possible, align tasks with team members' interests and passions. When individuals are engaged in work they enjoy, their motivation and productivity increase.

Encourage Autonomy: Empower team members by giving them autonomy in their roles. Trusting individuals to take ownership of their work fosters motivation and creativity.

Provide Opportunities for Growth: Offer professional development opportunities that align with team members' aspirations. Encourage participation in workshops, training sessions, and mentorship programs.

Recognize Achievements: Regularly acknowledge and celebrate individual and team achievements. Recognition boosts morale and reinforces a culture of appreciation.

Foster a Positive Work Environment: Create a supportive and positive work environment where team members feel safe to express their ideas and take risks. A positive atmosphere enhances motivation and engagement.

By understanding and addressing the diverse motivations of your team members, you can inspire them to perform at their best.

Conflict Resolution Strategies for a Harmonious Workplace

Conflict is a natural part of teamwork, but how it is managed can significantly impact team dynamics. Effective conflict resolution strategies foster a harmonious workplace and promote collaboration.

Tips for Resolving Conflicts:

Address Conflicts Early: Don't allow conflicts to fester. Address issues as soon as they arise to prevent escalation and maintain a positive work environment.

Listen Actively: When conflicts occur, practice active listening. Allow each party to express their concerns without interruption and show empathy for their perspectives.

Stay Neutral: As a leader, maintain neutrality during conflicts. Avoid taking sides and focus on facilitating a constructive discussion between the parties involved.

Encourage Collaborative Solutions: Invite conflicting parties to work together to find a mutually agreeable solution. Encourage brainstorming and compromise to reach a resolution that satisfies everyone involved.

Set Ground Rules: Establish ground rules for conflict resolution discussions, such as respecting each other's viewpoints and avoiding personal attacks. Clear guidelines help maintain a constructive atmosphere.

Follow Up: After resolving a conflict, follow up with the involved parties to ensure that the solution is working and that relationships are on the mend. This follow-up demonstrates your commitment to maintaining a harmonious workplace.

By implementing effective conflict resolution strategies, you can create a positive work environment that encourages collaboration and teamwork.

Creating Psychological Safety: Empowering Your Team to Take Risks

Psychological safety is essential for fostering innovation and creativity within a team. When team members feel safe to express their ideas and take risks, they are more likely to contribute their best work.

Strategies for Creating Psychological Safety:

Encourage Open Dialogue: Create an environment where team members feel comfortable sharing their thoughts and opinions. Encourage open discussions and welcome diverse perspectives.

Normalize Risk-Taking: Emphasize that taking risks is a valuable part of the learning process. Share examples of successful risk-taking within the organization to reinforce its importance.

Respond Constructively to Mistakes: When mistakes occur, focus on constructive responses rather than blame. Use errors as learning opportunities and encourage team members to analyze what went wrong and how to improve.

Model Vulnerability: As a leader, share your own experiences with failure and vulnerability. By demonstrating that it's okay to take risks and learn from mistakes, you encourage your team to do the same.

Celebrate Innovation: Recognize and celebrate innovative ideas and efforts, even if they don't result in success. Acknowledging creative attempts fosters a culture of experimentation and exploration.

Build Trust Through Consistency: Consistently demonstrate integrity and support for your team. When team members trust that their leader will advocate for them and support their initiatives, they feel safer taking risks.

Creating psychological safety within your team empowers individuals to take risks, share ideas, and contribute to a culture of innovation.

In this chapter, we've explored the essential elements of building high-performing teams, including fostering collaboration, effective delegation, meaningful feedback, motivation, conflict resolution, and creating psychological safety. By implementing these strategies, you can cultivate an empowered team that works collaboratively toward achieving shared goals. In the next chapter, we will delve into strategies for developing effective leadership styles that resonate with diverse teams.

Chapter 07

Mentorship and Sponsorship – Lifting as You Rise

MENTORSHIP AND SPONSORSHIP - LIFTING AS YOU RISE

In the journey of leadership, mentorship and sponsorship play pivotal roles in professional development and career advancement. While mentorship involves guidance and advice, sponsorship takes it a step further by advocating for individuals and opening doors to opportunities. This chapter will explore the differences between mentorship and sponsorship, how to cultivate these relationships, and the importance of giving back to the next generation of leaders.

The Difference Between Mentorship and Sponsorship, and Why You Need Both

Understanding the distinctions between mentorship and sponsorship is crucial for leveraging both effectively in your leadership journey.

Key Differences:

Mentorship: Mentorship typically involves a more informal relationship where a more experienced individual provides guidance, advice, and support to a less experienced person. This relationship focuses on personal and professional development, offering insights and perspectives that help mentees navigate challenges.

Sponsorship: Sponsorship goes beyond mentorship by actively promoting and advocating for an individual. A sponsor is usually a higher-level leader who uses their influence to create opportunities for their protégé, such as recommending them for promotions, high-visibility projects, or leadership roles.

Why You Need Both:

Comprehensive Support: While mentorship provides the guidance needed to develop skills and navigate challenges, sponsorship offers the strategic support necessary for advancing in your career. Both relationships are essential for building a robust professional network and achieving long-term success.

Diverse Perspectives: Having mentors and sponsors from diverse backgrounds can provide unique insights and broaden your understanding of different leadership styles, strategies, and approaches.

Accelerated Growth: Engaging with both mentors and sponsors can significantly accelerate your career growth, helping you overcome obstacles and seize opportunities that may not be accessible without their support.

How to Find and Approach Mentors and Sponsors

Finding the right mentors and sponsors is crucial for your professional development. Here are actionable steps to identify and approach potential mentors and sponsors.

Tips for Finding Mentors:

Identify Your Needs: Reflect on your career goals and the areas in which you seek guidance. This clarity will help you identify mentors whose experiences align with your objectives.

Look Within Your Network: Start by exploring your existing network, including colleagues, supervisors, and industry contacts. Seek individuals who have expertise in areas where you want to grow.

Attend Professional Events: Participate in conferences, workshops, and networking events relevant to your field. These settings provide opportunities to connect with potential mentors.

Leverage Social Media: Use platforms like LinkedIn to identify industry leaders and engage with their content. Comment on their posts or share insights to establish rapport before reaching out directly.

Approaching Mentors:

Be Genuine: When reaching out, express your admiration for their work and articulate why you believe they would be a good mentor. Be specific about what you hope to learn from them.

Be Respectful of Their Time: Acknowledge that potential mentors may have busy schedules. Suggest a brief meeting or coffee chat to discuss your interests and seek their advice.

Prepare Questions: Before meeting, prepare thoughtful questions to guide the conversation. This demonstrates your commitment to making the most of their time and expertise.

Finding Sponsors:

Demonstrate Your Value: To attract a sponsor, showcase your skills, accomplishments, and potential. Deliver consistent high-quality work and actively contribute to team success.

Build Relationships with Leaders: Engage with leaders in your organization or industry through projects, committees, or social events. Establishing rapport with decision-makers can lead to sponsorship opportunities.

Seek Feedback and Input: Regularly ask for feedback from leaders you aspire to connect with. This shows your willingness to learn and improve, increasing the likelihood that they will take notice of your potential.

Paying It Forward: Becoming a Mentor and Empowering Others

As you progress in your career, consider giving back by becoming a mentor to others. Mentorship is not only a way to support emerging leaders but also a powerful opportunity for personal growth and reflection.

Benefits of Being a Mentor:

Enhancing Leadership Skills: Mentoring others allows you to refine your leadership skills, including communication, empathy, and problem-solving.

Expanding Your Network: Mentoring can lead to new connections and opportunities, as your mentees may introduce you to their networks or collaborate on projects.

Creating a Legacy: By investing in the development of others, you contribute to a positive culture of support and empowerment within your organization or industry.

Tips for Becoming an Effective Mentor:

Be Approachable: Create an open and welcoming environment where mentees feel comfortable sharing their challenges and aspirations.

Listen Actively: Practice active listening and ask open-ended questions to encourage mentees to articulate their thoughts and concerns.

Share Your Experiences: Offer insights from your own journey, including successes and failures. Your experiences can provide valuable lessons for mentees navigating similar paths.

Encourage Independence: While providing guidance, encourage mentees to take ownership of their decisions and develop their problem-solving skills.

Stay Engaged: Check in regularly with your mentees, even after formal mentorship ends. Continued support reinforces your commitment to their growth.

By becoming a mentor, you can empower others to achieve their goals while also enhancing your own leadership capabilities.

How to Use Mentorship to Accelerate Career Growth

Mentorship can be a powerful catalyst for accelerating your career growth. By leveraging your mentorship relationships effectively, you can gain valuable insights and opportunities.

Strategies for Leveraging Mentorship:

Set Clear Goals: Establish specific goals for your mentorship relationship. What do you hope to achieve, and what skills do you want to develop? Share these goals with your mentor to guide your discussions.

Be Open to Feedback: Embrace constructive criticism and feedback from your mentor. Be willing to reflect on your strengths and areas for improvement, using their insights to fuel your growth.

Seek Opportunities for Exposure: Ask your mentor for introductions to their network or for opportunities to participate in high-visibility projects. Exposure to new experiences can significantly enhance your career trajectory.

Request Specific Advice: When faced with challenges, seek specific advice from your mentor. Frame your questions clearly to facilitate meaningful discussions that lead to actionable solutions.

Follow Through on Guidance: Implement the advice and strategies provided by your mentor. Demonstrating your commitment to applying their insights reinforces the value of the mentorship relationship.

Express Gratitude: Acknowledge and thank your mentor for their time and support. Acknowledgment fosters goodwill and strengthens the relationship.

The Role of Networking in Building Strong Leadership Relationships

Networking is a vital component of leadership development and career advancement. Building strong relationships through networking can open doors to mentorship and sponsorship opportunities.

Tips for Effective Networking:

Be Proactive: Take the initiative to reach out to individuals in your industry. Attend networking events, participate in online forums, and engage with thought leaders on social media.

Focus on Quality Over Quantity: Rather than trying to connect with as many people as possible, focus on building meaningful relationships with a select few. Depth of connection is often more valuable than breadth.

Follow Up: After meeting someone, follow up with a personalized message expressing your appreciation for the conversation. This helps reinforce the connection and keeps the lines of communication open.

Offer Value: Look for ways to offer value to your network. Whether sharing insights, providing introductions, or offering support, being a resource enhances your relationships.

Stay Connected: Maintain regular contact with your network by checking in periodically, sharing relevant articles, or inviting connections for coffee. Consistent engagement strengthens relationships over time.

Be Authentic: Approach networking with authenticity and a genuine interest in building relationships. People are more likely to connect with you when they sense your sincerity.

By actively engaging in networking, you can build a robust leadership network that supports your growth and opens doors to mentorship and sponsorship opportunities.

Strategies for Creating Your Own "Personal Board of Advisors"

A personal board of advisors is a group of trusted individuals who provide guidance, support, and diverse perspectives on your career journey. Creating a personal board can enhance your decision-making and leadership effectiveness.

Steps to Create Your Personal Board:

Identify Your Needs: Reflect on the areas where you seek guidance and support. Consider your career goals, challenges, and aspirations when determining the types of advisors you need.

Select Diverse Advisors: Choose individuals from different backgrounds, industries, and experiences to create a well-rounded board. This diversity will provide you with a variety of perspectives and insights.

Reach Out and Invite: Approach potential advisors with a clear explanation of why you value their expertise and how you envision the relationship. Be respectful of their time and express your genuine interest in their guidance.

Establish Expectations: Clearly communicate your expectations for the relationship, including how often you'd like to meet and the topics you wish to discuss. Setting clear boundaries helps manage the relationship effectively.

Engage Regularly: Schedule regular check-ins with your board members to seek advice, share updates, and discuss challenges. Consistent engagement fosters a supportive network.

Show Appreciation: Acknowledge and thank your advisors for their time and insights. Regularly expressing gratitude reinforces the value of the relationship and encourages continued support.

By creating a personal board of advisors, you build a support system that empowers you to navigate your leadership journey with confidence and clarity.

In this chapter, we've explored the critical roles of mentorship and sponsorship in leadership development, the importance of paying it forward, and actionable strategies for creating your personal board of advisors. By leveraging these relationships and engaging in networking, you can accelerate your growth as a leader in a changing world. In the next chapter, we will delve into the significance of lifelong learning and adaptability in effective leadership.

Part 3:
Building a Personal Brand as a Female Leader

Chapter 08

Work-Life Integration and Avoiding Burnout

In today's fast-paced world, the conversation around work-life balance is evolving. Instead of striving for an unattainable balance, many leaders are embracing the concept of work-life integration. This chapter delves into understanding this paradigm shift, establishing healthy boundaries, prioritizing self-care, managing time effectively, recognizing burnout, and implementing practical strategies for fulfillment in both professional and personal realms.

Understanding the Myth of "Work-Life Balance" and Striving for Integration

The traditional notion of work-life balance suggests that work and personal life are opposing forces that must be equally weighted. However, this perspective can create unrealistic expectations and added stress.

The Shift to Work-Life Integration:

Redefining Balance: Work-life integration acknowledges that work and personal life often overlap. Rather than aiming for a perfect equilibrium, focus on blending responsibilities and commitments in a way that suits your lifestyle.

Flexibility is Key: Embrace flexible work arrangements, such as remote work or flexible hours, that allow you to fulfill both personal and professional responsibilities without compromising one for the other.

Personal Priorities: Identify your core values and priorities in both work and personal life. By understanding what matters most to you, you can make more intentional decisions that align with your goals.

Fluidity: Recognize that your work-life integration will evolve over time due to changes in personal circumstances, career demands, or external factors. Be adaptable and willing to reassess your approach regularly.

By embracing work-life integration, you can create a more harmonious and fulfilling life, reducing the pressure to achieve an unrealistic balance.

How to Set Boundaries Without Guilt or Sacrificing Career Progress

Setting boundaries is essential for maintaining your well-being and ensuring that you can meet your personal and professional commitments. However, many women struggle with guilt when it comes to establishing these boundaries.

Steps to Establish Healthy Boundaries:

Identify Your Limits: Reflect on your personal and professional limits. What are your non-negotiables, and where do you feel overextended? Understanding these limits is the first step to setting effective boundaries.

Communicate Clearly: When setting boundaries, communicate them clearly to colleagues and supervisors. Be assertive yet respectful, explaining your need for balance without feeling the need to justify yourself.

Practice Saying No: Learn to say no to requests that conflict with your priorities or overextend your capacity. Saying no can be empowering and allows you to focus on what truly matters.

Schedule Downtime: Treat personal time with the same importance as work commitments. Schedule downtime, family activities, and self-care into your calendar to ensure you prioritize these moments.

Stay Consistent: Consistency is key in maintaining boundaries. Once established, stick to your boundaries to reinforce their importance, both to yourself and others.

Reassess as Needed: Regularly evaluate your boundaries to ensure they align with your evolving needs and circumstances. Be open to adjusting them as necessary.

By establishing and communicating boundaries, you can protect your time and energy while still making progress in your career.

Prioritizing Self-Care as an Essential Part of Leadership Success

Self-care is not a luxury; it's a necessity for effective leadership. Prioritizing self-care enables you to perform at your best, both personally and professionally.

Essential Self-Care Practices:

Physical Health: Engage in regular physical activity, eat balanced meals, and get adequate sleep. Physical health directly impacts mental clarity and emotional resilience.

Mental Wellness: Incorporate practices such as mindfulness, meditation, or yoga into your routine. These activities promote mental well-being and reduce stress.

Time for Hobbies: Make time for hobbies and interests outside of work. Engaging in activities that bring you joy can recharge your energy and enhance creativity.

Social Connections: Nurture relationships with friends, family, and mentors. Social support is vital for emotional health and provides a network to lean on during challenging times.

Regular Check-Ins: Schedule regular check-ins with yourself to assess your well-being. Reflect on what is working and what may need adjustment in your self-care routine.

Set Realistic Goals: Avoid overcommitting yourself. Set realistic goals that allow you to manage your time effectively while still prioritizing self-care.

By prioritizing self-care, you enhance your ability to lead effectively and maintain a healthy work-life integration.

Managing Time Effectively with the Demands of Leadership

Effective time management is critical for navigating the demands of leadership while maintaining work-life integration.

Time Management Strategies:

Prioritize Tasks: Use tools like the Eisenhower Matrix to prioritize tasks based on urgency and importance. Focus on what truly matters rather than getting caught up in minor details.

Block Time for Focus: Schedule dedicated blocks of time for focused work. Minimize distractions during these periods to maximize productivity.

Delegate Wisely: Delegate tasks that can be handled by others, allowing you to focus on higher-level responsibilities. Trusting your team to take on tasks empowers them and frees up your time.

Limit Multitasking: Multitasking can reduce efficiency and lead to mistakes. Focus on one task at a time to improve the quality of your work.

Use Technology: Leverage technology tools, such as calendar apps and project management software, to organize tasks, set reminders, and track deadlines effectively.

Establish Routines: Create daily routines that include time for work, self-care, and personal activities. Routines help establish structure and make it easier to manage time effectively.

By employing effective time management strategies, you can navigate leadership demands while maintaining a fulfilling personal life.

How to Recognize the Early Signs of Burnout and Address Them

Burnout is a state of physical, emotional, and mental exhaustion that can arise from prolonged stress and overcommitment. Recognizing the early signs of burnout is crucial for addressing it before it escalates.

Early Signs of Burnout:

Chronic Fatigue: If you frequently feel exhausted, even after a good night's sleep, this may be an early sign of burnout.

Decreased Motivation: A noticeable decline in motivation or enthusiasm for your work can indicate burnout. If tasks feel overwhelming, it may be time to reassess your commitments.

Increased Irritability: Feeling irritable or easily frustrated by colleagues or daily tasks can signal emotional exhaustion.

Difficulty Concentrating: Struggling to focus or experiencing "brain fog" can be a sign of burnout, impacting your productivity and effectiveness.

Physical Symptoms: Physical manifestations of stress, such as headaches, stomachaches, or changes in appetite, can also indicate burnout.

Withdrawal from Activities: A loss of interest in activities you once enjoyed, both at work and outside of it, may be a red flag.

Addressing Burnout:

Take Breaks: Schedule regular breaks throughout your day to recharge and refocus. Short breaks can significantly enhance productivity and well-being.

Evaluate Your Workload: Assess your current commitments and consider reducing responsibilities that contribute to burnout. Prioritize essential tasks and eliminate non-essential ones.

Seek Support: Talk to trusted colleagues, friends, or mentors about your feelings. Sharing your experiences can provide relief and new perspectives.

Practice Mindfulness: Incorporate mindfulness practices to reduce stress and promote mental clarity. Techniques such as deep breathing, meditation, or journaling can be effective.

Consider Professional Help: If burnout symptoms persist, consider seeking professional support from a therapist or counselor who specializes in workplace stress.

Engage in Enjoyable Activities: Make time for activities that bring you joy and relaxation. Engaging in hobbies or spending time with loved ones can help counteract burnout.

Recognizing and addressing the early signs of burnout is essential for maintaining both your well-being and your effectiveness as a leader.

Practical Strategies for Finding Fulfillment Both at Work and at Home

Achieving fulfillment in both your professional and personal life requires intentional effort and planning. Here are practical strategies to help you cultivate satisfaction in both areas.

Strategies for Finding Fulfillment:

Set Intentions: At the beginning of each week, set clear intentions for what you want to achieve at work and home. Intentions provide direction and help you stay focused on your priorities.

Create a Balanced Schedule: Design a schedule that allocates time for work commitments, family activities, and personal time. A balanced schedule helps ensure you dedicate time to what matters most.

Celebrate Small Wins: Acknowledge and celebrate small achievements, both at work and home. Recognizing progress boosts motivation and reinforces a sense of fulfillment.

Engage in Reflective Practices: Take time to reflect on your experiences regularly. Journaling or meditating can help you gain clarity on what brings you joy and fulfillment.

Foster Relationships: Invest in building and maintaining relationships with colleagues and loved ones. Strong connections enhance fulfillment and provide a support network during challenging times.

Be Present: Practice being present in the moment, whether at work or home. Mindfulness can help you fully engage in experiences, enhancing satisfaction and joy.

By implementing these strategies, you can find fulfillment in both your professional and personal life, leading to a more enriching and balanced existence.

In this chapter, we have explored the evolving concept of work-life integration, the importance of setting boundaries, prioritizing self-care, managing time effectively, recognizing burnout, and practical strategies for achieving fulfillment. Embracing these principles will empower you to thrive as a leader while maintaining a healthy and satisfying personal life. In the next chapter, we will discuss the significance of continuous learning and adaptability in effective leadership.

Chapter 09
Leading Through Change and Uncertainty

In an ever-evolving business landscape, the ability to lead through change and uncertainty has become a critical skill for effective leaders. This chapter explores the mindset needed for adaptability, strategies for guiding teams through transitions, effective communication techniques, the importance of transparency, resilience in the face of change, and the role of innovation in future-focused leadership.

How to Develop a Mindset of Adaptability and Flexibility

Adaptability is more than just a skill; it's a mindset that enables leaders to navigate changing environments effectively. Cultivating this mindset is essential for leading teams through uncertainty.

Steps to Foster Adaptability:

Embrace a Growth Mindset: Cultivate a belief that abilities and intelligence can be developed through dedication and hard work. A growth mindset encourages learning and resilience in the face of challenges.

Stay Informed: Keep abreast of industry trends, market shifts, and emerging technologies. Understanding the external landscape will prepare you to adapt quickly and effectively.

Encourage Experimentation: Foster a culture where experimentation is encouraged. Allow team members to test new ideas and learn from failures, reinforcing that adaptability is a valuable asset.

Reflect on Past Changes: Regularly reflect on previous changes you've navigated successfully. Analyze what worked and what didn't, using these insights to inform your approach to future changes.

Be Open to Feedback: Create an environment where feedback is welcomed. Listening to team members can provide diverse perspectives that enhance your adaptability and decision-making.

Practice Mindfulness: Engage in mindfulness practices that enhance self-awareness and emotional regulation. Being present helps you respond to change thoughtfully rather than react impulsively.

By developing a mindset of adaptability and flexibility, you can lead your team with confidence through periods of change and uncertainty.

Strategies for Leading Your Team Through Organizational Change

Leading a team through organizational change requires strategic planning and a supportive approach. Implementing effective strategies can help ease the transition and foster team cohesion.

Effective Strategies for Change Leadership:

Involve Your Team Early: Engage team members in the change process from the outset. Involving them in discussions and decisions fosters ownership and reduces resistance.

Set Clear Objectives: Clearly define the goals and reasons for the change. Providing context helps team members understand the necessity of the change and aligns their efforts.

Develop a Change Plan: Create a comprehensive change management plan that outlines the steps involved, timelines, and resources needed. A structured plan reduces ambiguity and guides the team through the transition.

Provide Training and Resources: Equip your team with the necessary training and resources to adapt to new processes or technologies. Continuous support reinforces confidence in their abilities.

Celebrate Milestones: Acknowledge and celebrate achievements throughout the change process, no matter how small. Recognizing progress keeps morale high and encourages continued commitment.

Be Approachable: Maintain an open-door policy, allowing team members to voice concerns or ask questions. Being approachable fosters trust and encourages open dialogue.

By employing these strategies, you can lead your team effectively through organizational change, ensuring they feel supported and engaged.

Communicating Effectively During Times of Uncertainty

Effective communication is vital during periods of uncertainty. How you convey information can significantly impact your team's confidence and morale.

Key Communication Practices:

Be Proactive: Don't wait for your team to ask for updates. Provide regular information about the change process, even if there's not much to share. Proactive communication reduces anxiety and speculation.

Use Clear Language: Avoid jargon and complex terminology. Use straightforward language that ensures your message is easily understood by all team members.

Encourage Questions: Create a safe space for team members to ask questions. Addressing their concerns openly fosters trust and demonstrates your commitment to transparency.

Utilize Multiple Channels: Use various communication channels, such as emails, team meetings, and one-on-one check-ins, to reach all team members effectively. Different individuals may prefer different methods of communication.

Share Personal Insights: Open up about your feelings regarding the changes. Sharing your own uncertainties humanizes your leadership and creates a sense of shared experience.

Follow Up: After communicating important information, follow up with your team to address any lingering questions or concerns. This reinforces your commitment to keeping lines of communication open.

By prioritizing effective communication, you can reduce uncertainty and foster a sense of stability within your team.

The Importance of Transparency and Honesty in Leadership Transitions

During transitions, transparency and honesty are essential for maintaining trust and credibility as a leader.

Practices for Fostering Transparency:

Share the Why: Clearly communicate the reasons behind the change. Understanding the rationale helps team members feel informed and engaged in the process.

Acknowledge Challenges: Don't shy away from discussing potential challenges and difficulties. Acknowledging these issues shows honesty and prepares your team for the realities of the transition.

Be Honest About Limitations: If there are uncertainties or limitations in the change process, be upfront about them. Honesty builds trust and encourages team members to voice their concerns.

Invite Feedback: Encourage team members to share their thoughts and opinions about the transition. Listening to their feedback demonstrates that their input is valued and considered in decision-making.

Maintain Consistency: Ensure that your messages remain consistent across different channels and forums. Inconsistent messaging can lead to confusion and erode trust.

Lead by Example: Model transparency in your own actions and communications. Your willingness to be open and honest sets the tone for your team's behavior.

By prioritizing transparency and honesty, you create a supportive environment where team members feel valued and informed during leadership transitions.

Staying Resilient and Grounded in the Face of Rapid Change

Change can be overwhelming, but cultivating resilience allows leaders to stay grounded and maintain focus.

Strategies for Building Resilience:

Cultivate Emotional Awareness: Regularly check in with your emotions and those of your team. Acknowledging feelings allows for better emotional regulation and fosters a supportive atmosphere.

Practice Self-Care: Prioritize self-care routines that enhance your physical and mental well-being. Engage in activities that recharge your energy and promote relaxation.

Maintain a Positive Outlook: Focus on the potential opportunities that change can bring rather than solely on the challenges. A positive mindset can influence your team's perceptions and reactions to change.

Build Strong Relationships: Foster relationships within your team and beyond. A supportive network provides resources, advice, and encouragement during challenging times.

Develop Problem-Solving Skills: Equip yourself and your team with effective problem-solving techniques. Being proactive in addressing challenges increases confidence in navigating change.

Embrace Flexibility: Recognize that change may require adjustments to your plans. Be open to altering your strategies as new information arises or circumstances shift.

By cultivating resilience, you can remain grounded and guide your team effectively through periods of rapid change.

The Role of Innovation and Creative Thinking in Future-Focused Leadership

In a rapidly changing environment, innovation and creative thinking are essential for effective leadership. Encouraging a culture of innovation can position your organization for future success.

Fostering Innovation and Creativity:

Encourage a Culture of Experimentation: Create an environment where team members feel safe to experiment and explore new ideas without fear of failure. Celebrating experimentation fosters a mindset of innovation.

Diverse Perspectives: Promote diversity within your team. Diverse perspectives lead to creative solutions and innovative approaches to challenges.

Provide Resources for Innovation: Allocate time and resources for team members to explore innovative ideas and projects. Encouraging creative endeavors can lead to breakthroughs that benefit the organization.

Facilitate Brainstorming Sessions: Organize regular brainstorming sessions to generate new ideas and encourage collaborative problem-solving. Foster an inclusive environment where all voices are heard.

Recognize and Reward Innovation: Acknowledge and reward innovative contributions from team members. Recognition motivates continued creativity and reinforces the importance of innovation within the organization.

Stay Curious: As a leader, maintain a curious mindset. Explore new trends, technologies, and practices that could enhance your organization's operations and strategies.

By embracing innovation and creative thinking, you can lead your team toward a future-focused approach that thrives in change.

In this chapter, we've explored the mindset of adaptability, strategies for leading through organizational change, effective communication practices, the importance of transparency, resilience in the face of change, and the role of innovation in leadership. As you continue to develop these skills, you will be better equipped to navigate the complexities of leadership in a rapidly changing world. In the final chapter, we will discuss the importance of continuous growth and the commitment to lifelong learning as essential elements of effective leadership.

Chapter 10
The Future of Women in Leadership

As we look ahead, the role of women in leadership continues to evolve, driven by cultural shifts, technological advancements, and the demand for diverse perspectives in decision-making. This chapter explores the future landscape for women leaders, offering insights into evolving roles, preparing for change, embracing technology, breaking barriers in male-dominated industries, building diverse leadership pipelines, and committing to lifelong learning and personal growth.

The Evolving Roles of Women Leaders in the 21st Century

The 21st century has ushered in new paradigms for leadership, and women are at the forefront of this transformation. As societal norms shift and organizations recognize the value of diverse leadership, women leaders are finding expanded opportunities and influence.

Key Trends Influencing Women's Leadership:

Increased Representation: More women are assuming leadership roles in various sectors, from politics to business. This increased representation not only challenges stereotypes but also serves as inspiration for future generations.

Diverse Leadership Styles: Women often bring collaborative and inclusive leadership styles that prioritize emotional intelligence, empathy, and relationship-building, leading to healthier workplace cultures and better team dynamics.

Focus on Work-Life Integration: As discussions around work-life balance evolve into work-life integration, women leaders are leveraging flexible work arrangements to support their careers and personal lives simultaneously.

Advocacy for Equality: Women leaders are increasingly advocating for equity in the workplace, driving initiatives that address gender bias and promote diversity at all organizational levels.

Mentorship and Sponsorship: The importance of mentorship and sponsorship is gaining recognition, with women supporting one another to navigate the complexities of leadership and career advancement.

Social Responsibility: Women leaders are often at the forefront of corporate social responsibility initiatives, prioritizing sustainability, ethical practices, and community engagement in their leadership approach.

As the roles of women leaders continue to evolve, they will play a crucial role in shaping the future of organizations and societies.

How to Prepare for Leadership in a Rapidly Changing Global Environment

The rapid pace of change in today's global environment requires leaders to be agile, informed, and adaptable. Preparing for this landscape involves strategic planning and a proactive approach to personal and professional development.

Steps for Effective Preparation:

Stay Informed: Regularly engage with industry trends, geopolitical developments, and economic shifts. Staying informed equips you to anticipate changes and respond strategically.

Develop Cross-Cultural Competence: As workplaces become more globalized, understanding different cultures and perspectives is essential. Invest time in learning about cultural dynamics and communication styles.

Enhance Adaptability: Cultivating a flexible mindset is critical for navigating uncertainty. Embrace change as an opportunity for growth rather than a challenge to be avoided.

Build a Diverse Network: Networking with individuals from various backgrounds and industries can provide new insights and foster collaborative opportunities. Diverse connections enhance your ability to lead in a global environment.

Engage in Scenario Planning: Anticipate potential future scenarios by engaging in scenario planning exercises. This proactive approach prepares you for various outcomes and enhances strategic thinking.

Invest in Personal Development: Commit to continuous personal and professional growth through workshops, courses, and conferences that focus on leadership skills, industry trends, and emerging technologies.

By preparing effectively for leadership in a rapidly changing global environment, you can position yourself and your organization for success.

Embracing Technology and Digital Leadership Skills

Technology is transforming the workplace, and effective leaders must embrace digital skills to thrive in this new landscape. Digital leadership encompasses not only the ability to use technology but also to leverage it for strategic advantage.

Essential Digital Leadership Skills:

Data Literacy: Understanding how to interpret and use data to inform decision-making is crucial. Leaders should cultivate data literacy to drive insights and optimize strategies.

Digital Communication: Mastering digital communication tools, such as video conferencing, collaborative software, and social media, enhances connectivity and engagement within teams.

Cybersecurity Awareness: Leaders must prioritize cybersecurity by understanding the risks associated with digital platforms and implementing measures to protect organizational data.

Agile Project Management: Familiarity with agile methodologies allows leaders to adapt quickly to changes, prioritize tasks effectively, and manage remote teams efficiently.

Innovative Mindset: Embracing innovation and being open to experimenting with new technologies can drive progress and enhance organizational competitiveness.

Lifelong Learning in Technology: The digital landscape is constantly evolving, making it essential for leaders to commit to lifelong learning to stay abreast of technological advancements and trends.

By embracing technology and developing digital leadership skills, women can navigate the complexities of modern leadership with confidence and competence.

Breaking into Traditionally Male-Dominated Industries

Despite progress, women still face challenges when breaking into industries traditionally dominated by men. However, with determination and strategic approaches, women can successfully carve their paths in these fields.

Strategies for Breaking Barriers:

Leverage Existing Networks: Utilize your existing network to gain insights and support when entering male-dominated industries. Seek mentorship from women who have navigated similar paths.

Build Technical Skills: Invest in acquiring technical skills relevant to your chosen industry. This expertise can enhance your credibility and position you as a valuable asset.

Advocate for Diversity: Be an advocate for diversity within your industry. Engage in discussions about the importance of diverse perspectives and the benefits they bring to organizations.

Challenge Stereotypes: Actively challenge stereotypes and biases in your industry by demonstrating competence and confidence. Your actions can help shift perceptions and pave the way for others.

Seek Out Supportive Environments: Identify organizations that prioritize diversity and inclusion. Joining companies with supportive cultures can significantly impact your career advancement.

Be Visible: Share your successes and insights within your industry. Visibility is crucial in breaking down barriers and inspiring other women to follow suit.

By employing these strategies, women can successfully break into and thrive in traditionally male-dominated industries.

Building and Sustaining Diverse Leadership Pipelines

Creating and sustaining diverse leadership pipelines is essential for fostering inclusive organizations that reflect the demographics of their communities and clients. Leaders play a pivotal role in this process.

Best Practices for Building Diverse Pipelines:

Commit to Diversity Goals: Establish clear diversity goals and objectives within your organization. Make these goals a priority in recruitment, retention, and promotion practices.

Implement Inclusive Hiring Practices: Review and revise hiring practices to eliminate bias. Consider using blind recruitment techniques and diverse interview panels to enhance inclusivity.

Provide Development Opportunities: Offer mentorship, sponsorship, and training programs tailored to underrepresented groups. Empowering individuals with skills and opportunities supports their leadership development.

Encourage Employee Resource Groups (ERGs): Support the establishment of ERGs to create safe spaces for employees from diverse backgrounds. These groups can foster community, networking, and advocacy within organizations.

Evaluate and Adjust Policies: Regularly assess organizational policies and practices to ensure they promote diversity and inclusivity. Make adjustments as needed to create a more supportive environment.

Celebrate Diverse Leaders: Highlight and celebrate the achievements of diverse leaders within your organization. Recognizing their contributions reinforces the value of diversity in leadership.

By actively building and sustaining diverse leadership pipelines, organizations can create a rich tapestry of perspectives that enhances decision-making and drives success.

Continuing Your Leadership Journey: Lifelong Learning and Personal Growth

Leadership is a continuous journey of learning and growth. Committing to lifelong learning not only enhances your skills but also prepares you to navigate future challenges.

Strategies for Lifelong Learning:

Pursue Professional Development: Invest in courses, certifications, and workshops that enhance your leadership skills and industry knowledge. Continuous education keeps you relevant and informed.

Engage in Self-Reflection: Regularly reflect on your experiences, successes, and areas for improvement. Self-reflection fosters self-awareness and informs your leadership style.

Seek Feedback: Actively seek feedback from colleagues and mentors to gain insights into your strengths and areas for growth. Constructive feedback can guide your development journey.

Network with Other Leaders: Build relationships with fellow leaders across various industries. Networking provides opportunities for knowledge-sharing and collaboration.

Stay Curious: Cultivate a curious mindset by exploring new topics, industries, and perspectives. Lifelong learners remain open to new ideas and experiences.

Prioritize Personal Well-Being: Remember that personal growth includes well-being. Prioritize self-care to maintain the energy and enthusiasm needed for effective leadership.

By committing to lifelong learning and personal growth, you can continuously evolve as a leader, ready to embrace the challenges and opportunities that lie ahead.

In this chapter, we've explored the evolving roles of women leaders, strategies for preparing for a rapidly changing environment, the importance of embracing technology, breaking into male-dominated industries, building diverse leadership pipelines, and the commitment to lifelong learning. As women continue to rise and thrive in leadership roles, the future holds promise for greater equity, innovation, and success in organizations worldwide.

Conclusion

Leading with Purpose, Passion, and Power

As we come to the close of Leadership for Women: Rise and Thrive, it's essential to reflect on the journey we've taken together and consider how to apply the lessons learned. Throughout this book, we have delved into the critical challenges women face in the modern workplace and explored the strategies necessary to navigate and overcome them.

Leadership, at its core, is not just about achieving personal goals or gaining professional accolades. It's about creating impact, inspiring others, and paving the way for future generations. Now, more than ever, women are standing at the helm of change, transforming industries, breaking down systemic barriers, and reshaping leadership in the process. This is your moment to rise, thrive, and lead with confidence, empathy, and resilience.

The Power of Your Leadership Journey

Every woman's leadership journey is unique. Whether you are a new leader, an aspiring professional, or someone who has led for decades, your path holds the potential to influence not only your organization but also the people who look up to you. The power of your journey lies in your ability to lead authentically and to bring your full self to every challenge, every decision, and every success.

The key takeaways from this book emphasize that effective leadership today requires a combination of emotional intelligence, strategic thinking, resilience, and integrity. It also demands the courage to overcome historical and societal barriers, the wisdom to lead with purpose, and the dedication to building diverse, high-performing teams.

How to Continue Building on the Skills Learned in This Book

The skills and insights gained from this book are not finite; they should be continuously cultivated and applied in various contexts.

The Changing Landscape of Leadership: A Call to Action

Leadership today looks different than it did even a decade ago. The traditional top-down approach is giving way to more collaborative, inclusive styles that value emotional intelligence and open communication. This shift creates immense opportunities for women who naturally excel in these areas. As a leader, you are not only shaping your personal success but also contributing to this broader transformation.

Now is the time to seize those opportunities. As women leaders, we are called upon to:

Embrace diversity and inclusion: The future of leadership is diverse. It requires that we build inclusive workplaces where every voice is heard, and every individual feels empowered to contribute.

Challenge gender biases: Systemic biases are still present in many industries. By challenging these biases—both within ourselves and our organizations—we can break down the barriers that have long held women back from leadership positions.

Support and lift others: Leadership is about bringing others along with you. Mentorship, sponsorship, and creating opportunities for the next generation of women leaders is crucial for long-term change.

The responsibility of leadership extends beyond your own career. It touches the lives of everyone you influence—whether directly through your work or indirectly as a role model. The choices you make as a leader today will ripple outwards, shaping the culture of the workplace and the opportunities available to future generations.

Final Thoughts on the Importance of Community and Collaboration for Women in Leadership

Overcoming Challenges and Building Resilience

Leadership is not without its challenges, especially for women. From imposter syndrome to navigating workplace politics, the obstacles can be significant. But as this book has shown, they are not insurmountable.

The women who thrive in leadership are those who build resilience in the face of these challenges. Resilience is the ability to bounce back from setbacks, learn from failure, and continue moving forward with determination. It is an essential trait for any leader, but it is particularly important for women who must often navigate unique challenges in the workplace.

The key to building resilience is to:

Cultivate self-awareness: Understand your strengths and areas for growth. This will allow you to make strategic decisions that align with your values and goals.

Seek mentorship and support: Surround yourself with people who can offer guidance, encouragement, and perspective. Mentors and sponsors play a crucial role in helping you navigate challenges and accelerate your growth.

Embrace failure as a learning opportunity: Every setback is a chance to learn and improve. Instead of seeing failure as a reflection of your abilities, view it as an opportunity to grow stronger.

Creating a Lasting Legacy

As women leaders, we have the unique opportunity to create a lasting legacy—not just through our individual achievements, but through the positive impact we have on others. This legacy is built on the principles of collaboration, empathy, and empowerment.

Creating a lasting legacy means:

Mentoring the next generation: Leadership is about lifting others as you rise. By mentoring and sponsoring emerging leaders, you ensure that your knowledge, skills, and insights are passed on.

Fostering a culture of innovation: Encourage creativity and innovation within your teams. Leaders who foster a culture of experimentation and open-mindedness will drive their organizations to new heights.

Promoting diversity and inclusion: Leaders who champion diversity and inclusion create environments where all individuals can thrive, regardless of their background or identity.

Your leadership legacy is about more than what you accomplish in your career—it's about how you make others feel, how you inspire them, and how you contribute to creating a better, more inclusive world.

The Journey Continues

Leadership is not a destination; it is an ongoing journey of growth, learning, and adaptation. The insights and strategies in this book are meant to guide you, but the true work begins when you apply these lessons to your everyday leadership.

As you continue your leadership journey, remember that every decision, every challenge, and every success shapes the future of women in leadership. You are not just leading for yourself; you are leading for the generations of women who will follow in your footsteps.

The path forward is clear: lead with purpose, passion, and power. Rise, thrive, and leave a legacy that will inspire others for years to come.

Closing Thoughts

The future of leadership is bright, and women are at the forefront of that change. With the tools and strategies provided in this book, you are now equipped to take on the challenges of leadership with confidence and resilience.

As you move forward in your leadership journey, keep this in mind: You have the power to create positive change. Your leadership has the potential to transform organizations, inspire others, and pave the way for a more equitable and inclusive future.

It's time to rise. It's time to thrive. And it's time to lead.

www.ingramcontent.com/pod-product-compliance
Lightning Source LLC
Chambersburg PA
CBHW050307230526
45471CB00005B/2065